THE NATIONAL POETRY SERIES

The National Poetry Series was established in 1978 to ensure the publication of five collections of poetry annually through five participating publishers. The Series is funded annually by Amazon Literary Partnership, Betsy Community Fund, the Gettinger Family Foundation, Bruce Gibney, HarperCollins Publishers, Stephen King, Lannan Foundation, Newman's Own Foundation, News Corp, Anna and Olafur Olafsson, the O. R. Foundation, the PG Family Foundation, the Poetry Foundation, Laura and Robert Sillerman, Amy R. Tan and Louis De Mattei, Elise and Steven Trulaske, and the National Poetry Series Board of Directors.

2017 COMPETITION WINNERS

The Lumberjack's Dove by GennaRose Nethercott,
chosen by Louise Gluck for Ecco

Anarcha Speaks by Dominique Christina,
chosen by Tyehimba Jess for Beacon Press

feeld by Jos Charles,
chosen by Fady Joudah for Milkweed Editions

What It Doesn't Have to Do With by Lindsay Bernal,
chosen by Paul Guest for University of Georgia Press

Museum of the Americas by J. Michael Martinez,
chosen by Cornelius Eady for Penguin Books

What It Doesn't Have to Do With

What It Doesn't Have to Do With

POEMS BY LINDSAY BERNAL

The University of Georgia Press   ATHENS

Published by the University of Georgia Press
Athens, Georgia 30602
www.ugapress.org
© 2018 by Lindsay Bernal
All rights reserved
Designed by Kaelin Chappell Broaddus
Set in 10/13 Quadraat Regular by Kaelin Chappell Broaddus

Most University of Georgia Press titles are
available from popular e-book vendors.

Printed digitally

Library of Congress Cataloging-in-Publication Data

Names: Bernal, Lindsay, 1979– author.
Title: What it doesn't have to do with: poems / by Lindsay Bernal.
Other titles: What it does not have to do with
Description: Athens : The University of Georgia Press, [2018] |
 Series: The national poetry series | Includes bibliographical references.
Identifiers: LCCN 2018003969| ISBN 9780820353944 (pbk. : alk. paper) |
 ISBN 9780820353951 (ebook)
Classification: LCC PS3602.E75925 A6 2018 | DDC 811/.6—dc23
 LC record available at https://lccn.loc.gov/2018003969

For Nate
&
In Memory of
Otgontuul Bernal
(1978–2007)

CONTENTS

I.

Heartbroken in Your Memoir   3
The Pre-Raphaelite Effect   4
Postcard from Long Island City   8
Instead of Watching the Patriots   9
Interrogation after *The Cremaster Cycle*   10
An Early Nude by Rothko   11
Postcard from the Villa Catullo   12

II.

Fin de Siècle   15
Apologia   19
Femme Maison   20
Venice Is Sinking   21
Vessel   24
Broken Shoe   26
Before the Catastrophe   27
What It Doesn't Have to Do With   29
Aubade for Morrissey   30

III.

The Story of Our Estrangement   33
Rodin's Fallen Caryatid   34
No Echo   35
On Happiness   47
Twachtman's *Springtime*   48
Blossom Road   49

IV.

Summer in Kittery   53
Dolor Notebook   54
Lovebird   58
Widow   59
On Gardening and Geeshie Wiley   61
Not Going to Nova Scotia   62
Epithalamion for Nate   63
Sunset Redux   64
Postcard from Mazunte   65

Acknowledgments   67
Notes   69

I.

Heartbroken in Your Memoir

Thank you for immortalizing me
in half a sentence while you, the protean

go-getter, feed me soup, jasmine-tip tea.
If I were to meet my 21-year-old self

now, I'd never befriend her, but you fell into my lap—
literally—the night Ryan drugged us & I begged you

to get me the hell out of Lowell.
Thank you for that & for your Lady-of-Shallot look,

for being the only girl I kissed at the lesbian party
we'd waited all fall for, somewhere

on the Lower East Side, almost too east
to count back then—when Queens was still cheap,

my life a milky white, opaque & vague.
Who among us hadn't been compromised:

one morning waking up saying to nobody,
how did *that* happen? Then walking home

in the same clothes we'd laid out
the day before, in shoes not meant for distances

or daylight, past everyone with headsets
commuting to Wall. After six months

you left & I moved to the R's last stop,
my apartment so close to the tracks it shook.

The Pre-Raphaelite Effect

1

Midafternoon, the hum of porn fills the room:
        a redhead in a diaphanous catsuit
(love-bite on her breast-swell),
fearing no bondage,
                no slap of the whip.
Foreplay and more foreplay and a song sung on the soundtrack.
"Amber Lemons is from Jersey, not Malibu,
        went to Catholic School."
How do you know that?
Then she comes twice
        nose-down like a small animal
        in faux grass by the kidney-shaped pool.
Is she faking? Is she faking?

2

Paramour—that's what I'd like to be called.
If we hadn't skipped so many steps at the start
you'd know my mom is part French.
And *hate* isn't as simpleminded as you think.
My hatred of Ruskin's landscapes, for instance,
is fairly sophisticated: although no women appear in them
I see poor Effie Gray in every sunset,
in every godforsaken river and ruin.
Sometimes the autobiography just creeps in.
I'm glad, after John rejected her,
that Effie was able to recover and marry again.
No, I've never tried cuttlefish or finished *The Stones of Venice*
but several years back I wept watching *Summertime*.
Maybe if I were older or from the Midwest,
like Katharine Hepburn's character.
Adultery is always easier in the movies.

3

At the Apollo Diner some terms are too nebulous.
Some confessions are meant to be written

in permanent marker in a public restroom.
John is a popular name.

Last night I fell asleep with one hand
pressed against the wall for balance

and woke to a pain shooting through my arm.
If only I'd practiced more restraint at that bar.

In retrospect I should've put down my foot.
In retrospect you're an open book:

sooner or later you'll pour the same
Beam down some other girl's throat.

4

Yes, if she weren't grinning, she'd resemble Jesus:
sheet-white, contorted, less busty than usual.
Where does the light come from? The candelabrum holds
only dead wicks and stumps of wax.
Do you keep this place frigid on purpose
so her nipples stay erect?
A commissioned artist can afford utilities, especially one
already "risen" according to that important critic.
No windows, no books but Kerouac,
who doesn't count. Vintage pinups on the carpet.
And too much time spent wasted, wasting away.
When she closes her eyes, where does her mind go?
Fruit bowl, stain on the floor, fruit stain, somewhere far.

5

Something there is that doesn't love melodrama.

When you said you finally understood Botticelli
we were sitting close on the Dogana steps.

That was four years ago: I'd panicked,
then missed the train to Munich.

The things we want to forget we can't.

A long time I stood on the Bridge of Sighs,
waiting for the water to answer back.

But all I'd planned to say anyway was congrats!—
the wife, the kid, the grant.

6

A whole planet, like the face of a goddess,
        silhouetted against the sun
                just under 20 minutes:

the duration of *Jeopardy!* without commercials,
        coffee with Mom, my commute home.
                —But the precise moment of contact,

when Venus first touches the sun's edge,
        is impossible to discern
                and the separation's a blur

—what the folks at astrologyzone.com
        have termed the "teardrop."
                Who knows who touched who first?

So when I realized I missed it,
        that rare cosmic event that could cure
                every sexual hang-up,

I cried hard
        on the subway, on the crosstown bus,
                on a lonely park bench

overlooking the Hudson.
        A grown woman behaving like a child.
                I knew better than to harm myself,

I knew my loss was small
        in the larger scheme of things,
                in this city where every second

someone dies, another gives birth.
        My head between my knees,
                I couldn't take the onslaught

of spring, my part in it:
        the trees' showy leaves,
                the flowers slowly opening.

Postcard from Long Island City

The thing is I kept thinking
it would pass, this thickness
at the back of my mouth,
what shame tastes like
or vinegar. When Frank
wanted us both at once
I almost caved. You were shaking
your head. In a green mist
rising from the rooftop pool
I was of another mind
altogether. What I need
to say about that year
a note stuck on the fridge
couldn't begin to contain.
Today: inexorable
rain, wind that left
my cheeks chapped, burning,
but I didn't call in
sick or arrive late.
On the broken record player
I've piled more of your mail,
junk mostly, a few bills.
The jasmine plant is dying.
After I tried to suffocate you
with the goose down pillow
I felt awful. Like a woman
I'd seen in a Hopper:
at her bedroom window,
naked, except for a pair
of black flats.

Instead of Watching the Patriots

for the thousandth time, I'm reading Stein under an afghan,
    the one about hats.
I can't remember the half-time show or who won, but the last
    Super Bowl party I went to was 2002—
the day after, I lost my job and the day after that—Tuesday—
    I was proposed to outside a shitty bar
in Sunnyside. A whole hour in sleet with my head exposed
    waiting for him to arrive
stoned. The bouncer witnessed it—my shame a cliché
    stretched from neck to hairline.
I'd never felt so afraid of what I could accept, become: inert
    and fat
in the bare-bulb light of his basement apartment, a part of the
    couch, a pair of bloodshot eyes unable to read—
or worse, I'd end up like Alice Toklas slicing the meatloaf,
    filling the absinthe glass, packing and unpacking suitcases.
No way, absolutely not. In truth I hated the new color scheme:
    bright red kitchen,
bathroom as blue as the sky would never be, the dull liberty bell
    wallpaper soon to be peeled off
so we could paint the bedroom predictably. After the third
    vodka,
when I told him I felt tender, I meant in the stomach, not in the
    abstract.

Interrogation after *The Cremaster Cycle*

Do you have epic ambitions? Does the thought of your testicles descending and so much Vaseline make you queasy?

When you rose from the sofa, left the one-bedroom your dead friend left you to enter the overexposed photograph

of Fifth Avenue, one o'clock, did the winter sun shock you?

(If only you'd finished at Tisch or the band had survived the autumn slump—

Miles and his Napoleon complex and the problem of too much dope, not enough square feet or scapegoats.)

You want to rewind, start over? Bed-wetting, middle school, mysterious pangs?

Look at your companions reflected in the Plexiglas—soulless, forgettable,

or could you swear you recognize somebody from some show in Bushwick?

Did you flash her a cool smile, then wilt?

Was it her laugh that drew you or the way her skin glittered through the smoke?

Yes, the Guggenheim's always packed, even on weekdays.

Would you rather be stuck on the Isle of Man with Marti Domination or Ursula Andress?

No, Björk's not an option.

An Early Nude by Rothko

If her body seems both jagged and vague
sometimes waiting too long does that:
she dozes dog-faced, her proportions wrong,
all legs, the supple legs that kept you closer to her,
uncomfortably close on the brown vinyl chaise,
while the fan did little to lift the weight
of August, the clouds dragging the whole sky down
onto the street where you live together. Her busy head's
half on a pillow, half in the crook of her arm,
one dream or jerk away from falling off
the chaise, striking the end table's sharp corner
as she did once as a girl. *So much blood*,
she'd said, on her bedroom rug, how
her father had had to restrain her for the stitches.
How many times you've licked that chicken-scratch scar.
She's facing the wall, still nicotine-yellow
from the prior owner, and you want to press her
hard against it, break open the plaster,
or you want to leave through the back door
without waking her. Why always those galoshes,
even after she's slipped out of her papery sundress
spotted now with the rain that made this morning hotter.

Postcard from the Villa Catullo

From the Hotel Eden I could hardly distinguish
between the lake and the sky. It was that sunny.
What do I love and where are you? Fragments—
no, pesto—and you're in the Cinque Terre eating it.
I guess our relationship was meant to stay
platonic. Sapphire, cobalt, cyanine:
so many words for something impalpable.
Did you have a real cool time at the discotheques?
The bird Lesbia caressed, pressed to her chest, is dead,
but yesterday I looked and looked for it regardless
beyond Riva's cloudy peak. Then I drank a Coke.
In the ruins I smoked half a pack of Dunhills.
Since you left, I've been to paradise. I'm broke again.

II.

II.

Fin de Siècle

Weren't you always deplaning somewhere warm
with different hair & no job

beyond a less-than-part-time gig
tutoring a dilettante for 1,200 pesetas a week,

all of which you'd waste
with your imagined slam piece,

someone cruel said—a composite
of wants, really. (He loved the Latvian

bartender-model who ate only lemon wedges
dusted with salt.) At twenty, the turn of a century,

you chose a life without texture,
a half-dark, predictable plot.

The elevator to your host mom's flat
smelled like bleach or what bleach tries to block.

*

During the breakup talk,
when he said *your melancholy,*

you heard a contraction
(you *are*) instead of what he meant

& threw a plate. Those days
you couldn't see

Hemingway's misogyny,
sought him out.

Love has changed
says your dying matriarch

who grew up on a dairy farm
that's now an airport.

Why buy the cow when the milk's free?

*

A friend texts that her fetus
kicks her hardest, wildly, right after orgasm.

For the life of you
you can't muster a response. *Haha*

you finally text back,
followed by the hotdog emoji

(a mistake). She's the kind
who writes poems about being suckled

raw, "wet with milk in Starbucks,"
always writing while walking,

chai in one hand,
tram in the other.

*

The model becomes a peach,
a woman waiting for what.

Her hands cover her genitals
from behind & underneath

but Man Ray leaves her ass exposed,
a portal bathed in soft light.

Tender or horrific?
As you exit the exhibit

you feel manhandled,
not moved.

*

Or cell phone service is stalled
again & again, not one neighbor

you know. The guys at the 24-hour
car wash on 4th gone

& gone the false Polaris
of their neon sign

on your stroll home from the Slope.
No traffic at all

now that the ecstatic
sun's gone too.

What to do in a blackout?
Masturbate? Down

this pint of pistachio
before it spoils, before

the Milky Way & Cassiopeia
redden the horizon.

*

Fuck Nick & his body like a rock,
his paratactic problems

across a big two-hearted river.
You have one heart

& one's enough. Two-minded
would be better, more spiritual.

You were in the Tyrol or Lowell
when you figured out your body.

Did you shout from a mountain
or fire escape, *I have a body & it is useful?*

You remember stowing your bag
above your seat, showing some skin,

a glimpse of belly,
everyone's eyes on you.

Apologia

I'm sorry I subjected you to such bad art
that rainy morning you left me

—as bad, I think, as that wisp of a woman's
performance on Governor's Island:

she drank pink lemonade, then urinated
through her tights & tutu over & over.

I didn't get it, but she sure was beautiful
in her cube on a swivel chair, on the floor

resting or stretching her lithe body
like a cat, yogic, wholly dismissive

of her hipster audience. Me?
I was crouched in a corner of our home

unable to stop the flood.
Not even by swaddling myself

could I sufficiently diminish the I.
Nothing's less arousing than a woman

weeping, a bird confused by the weather.
The street cat hasn't been ravished yet

to which she, too, will respond by crying
just like the toddler next door

whining without end while I fake-sleep—
which is it? A child not trained

to self-soothe or routine cat-rape,
his barbed part inside for far too long.

Femme Maison

after Louise Bourgeois

Head in a whole leaky house
bought at auction, Masson's bird-caged

mannequin reinvented with two sons
in diapers, a gold-plated cross

around her neck that's strained
under all the brick, the immense

mansard roof needing repair,
needing paint, they, all three of them,

listening for the drips. The thickness
of the curtains bugs her most.

They block the sun, so rare here,
and part of her but not the wet.

Too much mind-clutter to work
and no spine, her mother's voice now

entering her head—house.
What makes her tragic, self-defeating,

to her own children even,
is that she doesn't know she's exposed,

half-naked. She's caught hiding
but doesn't know from what.

Venice Is Sinking

and so am I—into this wrought-iron chair—
distracted by laundry, a stranger's blouse blown stiff,

and my own mosquito-wrecked legs: that's what I get
for getting lost in the half-light.

There was a rushed introduction, the Giudecca
slack, sky-colored. No, I've never been attached

(infatuated, yes, but not attached). I ditched Dawn,
my only friend, when the Carabinieri

caught wind of her hash. Or I broke a glass—
not in anger, by accident, a tongue in my ear.

Then the crowd disappeared with the pigeons
that would eat from my hands if I let them.

*

Between Pound and Olga, the violinist,
is a lush laurel I watered with wine.

For him the laurel means enlightenment
even in San Michele, where there are no woods,

a shrub here and there by a gravestone,
but for me—the state I entered *was* tree-like:

I was lying on my back on my hands,
I didn't ask for it, my head

floating farther and farther away.
I was counting backward from a thousand in Italian

and on the grass a dirty skirt.

*

As the vaporetto passed San Vio's soap-smooth posts,
I nearly tossed myself over. Another *A Lume Spento*.

*

With tapers quenched, I walked out
of the dream I was stuck in.

O moon my pin-up,
how I wish I were a woman frescoed

in a loose dress, pulled by the hair
to heaven. Or Titian's voluptuous Virgin

rising above everyone who tries to touch her.
Red gown, blue shawl, her gaze always God-ward

she can't bear to look down.

*

I blame the diaphanous water,
the way the light struck my face.

Outside Wagner, afternoon bells.
No, not forlorn

—nauseous on a mosaic floor,
unmoved by the view

a caged man once longed for:
Santa Maria dei Miracoli's jewel-box façade,

the limestone siren with her nipple up
touching herself.

Yes, beauty is difficult.
And some days are dreadful without wind or rain

or paradise painted at the end.

Vessel

Jen says she's
an inadequate one

on bed rest
for months.

The weaker vessel,
according to the nuns

who taught me
every subject

from first grade onward.
Sisters of Saint Joseph,

founded by six women
in a small kitchen

in 17th-century Le Puy:
among them, an orphan,

of course, a lost
15-year-old,

a war widow.
Is that (widow-turned-

nun) even allowed?
In Rochester I'd known only

the opposite, failed nuns
who married, then sent

their girls to my school.
During the French Revolution

this congregation of women
fell apart, their convents

confiscated.
Many became

martyrs, guillotined
in honor of God

or maybe Mary in Dauphine.
That transatlantic journey

postrevolution must have been endless.
How many had scurvy?

How many died
en route to New Orleans

aboard the *Natchez*
as vulnerable a vessel as any?

How many looked up
at the sky each night

never more aware
of its emptiness?

Broken Shoe

White dress, one foot bare, sky on the verge of rain
in a city where the sky seems always on the verge of rain
with nothing to toss into the river but this busted slingback,
my underwear wadded at the bottom of my bag.
On a hard walk centuries before Vivier invented stilettos,
Mary Hamilton broke the heel off her shoe.
That detail appears in most versions of the ballad
but not in the one sung by Baez,
who didn't bother with shoes at all
and never smoked anything, never drank
her way into trouble or forgetting.
(In my head she's biting a Red Delicious,
slapping her Adam's apple to improve her vibrato.)
Everything went wrong for her, for Mary Hamilton, I mean.
And courtship is the worst: one minute you're splitting
steak frites, falling for the oldest tricks in the book,
and the next, you're back at his place flat on the floor,
knowing that the night will amount only to morning.

Before the Catastrophe

I wasn't trying to be erotic
though the presence of two figures

might imply that, their wild
springtime acrobatics

in a public lot downtown,
his arm under her skirt.

Do I want to be lusted after?
More than loved or liked.

Is this house real
because I made it?

Is it mine? Are there windows
without blinds?

For years I was one
immersed in

an otherwise empty
shotgun setup,

the rooms moving with
& through me

freely as I ate.
I braided my hair

then tied it in a knot,
soaked but rarely bathed

in the claw-foot tub.
Nobody who saw me gave a damn.

Before the catastrophe
(marriage, *Maman*, et cetera)

there was self
& self, my fleeting

unchangeable nature,
a pressure on me forever

to lose, elude
—you.

What It Doesn't Have to Do With

Not sleeping, not sleeping together, rain,
the villain from a post-Gothic romance
you've never read, the fake fireplace I'm in front of.
That chick you met at Johnson & Wales, who claims to be
half-gypsy, is irrelevant entirely. I could care less about her killer
risotto. If we weren't born jealous
we'd be happier more often. If my face weren't blank
you could tell me to wipe that look off it.

We've reached a juncture that deserves expression,
an ultimatum, something hurtful uttered in a hush.
The mouse I've just named Heathcliff skitters under the couch
but I'm too disappointed to stand on my chair.
Building nothing out of something.
The story's the same in the track that's skipping:
in the dark, in summer, a little drunk, everything looks better.
A big decision rushed. Another. Then the weather, then the weather.

Aubade for Morrissey

Again it's the caustic dog trainer, her
predawn shrieks cutting through the oaks

in Malcolm X Park, through Jeanne d'Arc too,
recoiling deeper into her bronze body,

the one woman on horseback in all of D.C.—
maybe the only *real* woman

among the eroticized virtues, fecund in some circle
or flanking a man-made pond.

In her right hand the recovered sword—
stolen in the seventies—in her left the reins,

she's off-kilter, twisted, frozen in forward motion
at nineteen, staring blindly at her future

or into the flamy sun as it melts over the condos
that obscure the Capitol, the earthquaked

obelisk. While three rescues learn to sit, heel,
I wake in a pool of want. My head out the window by now,

I face the same park I walked through all night
at Jeanne's age, brave with booze, believing

in nothing and not in love.

III.

The Story of Our Estrangement

after I don't apologize that time in the backyard
after the doctor staples your head shut & Mom moves
all the snow shovels to the highest shelf
after I sulk upstairs without supper
whispering the same three prayers
after the last shade is drawn the dead bolt locked
after I fall asleep easily after all that
years before you slug that girl in the stomach
with such vigor you knock the wind out of her
before I kiss Emily Elker just for practice under the big sumac
before I smoke Dad's cigarettes at the Barn Swallow cul-de-sac
before you're doing God knows what
in your bedroom the whole summer
Today's Tom Sawyer he gets high on you
blaring from your boom box
before I'm taking shots in the locker room with Cheryl
at the deserted playground waiting for those guys to show up
before I find my clitoris before someone we know slits her wrists
& Sister Miriam announces it on the loudspeaker
before you learn to drive
before you barrel through a red light totaling the Volvo
before I learn to drive all the way to Niagara Falls
but tell Mom I'm at the mall
when I have a run-in with a state trooper in Troy
when I think too long about Freud
when I realize how little you have to do with this
seeing you only on Christmas or less
when I feel alone when I'm not alone
when the moon looks far when the moon looks close

Rodin's Fallen Caryatid

She's collapsing under her big stone:
woe, love, whatever. Vase, urn, bowl,

the cup made of hands at the brook
—what holds is hollow.

Does a child ever recover
from losing the vessel who bore her,

pushed her out of one watery world into this?

Is it an image of damnation?
A grave woman contorted,

knocked over. And yet
we see her grace, her goddess-

smooth curves yielding to the earth.
Is it the stone—what she holds—

or the weight of her hollow body that betrays her?

No Echo

Was the wind wild through the trees (sumac,
rank tulip), full-of-voices alive—I mean,

did the mind win or did the body?
He lost the one he wanted to lie down beside

often without even speaking,
her hand in his, listening to her breathe,

feeling the first kicks of sleep.
Was her limbic system flawed

from the beginning or did it just combust?
Like a house on fire, all windows splintering at once,

or an idea gleaming into being.

*

Murder. *Of the self,* a colleague added as if I hadn't understood, his eyes widening, filling up the room. I shut my door. For several months I was like that, held by my grief or violated by it, looking past everyone I met, focused on the periphery, the filmy edges. The dream, what my mind saw, was clearer. The more time passed the more detailed and exact that day became. The handkerchief she used to mask the clock—white, embroidered with pale yellow flowers—to stop time or to hide her reflection in the clock's face. My younger brother, making his way from Midtown to Inwood, forgot where their apartment was. Ambulance, fire truck, two cop cars futilely wailing, the whole place a crime scene—investigated, swabbed, photographed—caution tape and all. And my older brother, the widower, interrogated, hysterical.

*

For sparrows the nest can be a desperate place:
at any moment a house wren can alight, attack the whole hatch.

They fledge because they have no choice
but to fly from it.

*

Twice in one year I've worn this outfit:
herringbone, pearls. How boring

to think the universe owed me the time
it takes to accept one loss before it dished out

another—as if the universe owes us anything.
The Sunday visits to the columbarium

among thousands who died with honor.
Gunshots. Drum. Taps. What I wanted to read

before the Tibetan monk's chant, after my brother's stoic
hello to everyone here today to honor my wife—

now like a doll, a dull made-up face
hovering above the casket—was rejected.

That a suicide could return to earth
not misshapen or blind, as the Buddhists believe,

lost on a crowded street, forced to beg
her way into the next life, but rather

as Indian paintbrush, fireweed: a shock of red
against eroded hillsides, able to thrive

however briefly beyond the tree line.

*

Not wet with dew but dust-swept,
trace of tear-stain. Why weep?

In this deaf desert, the dawn's
rawer and redder longer.

I squat to smell her,
smell mutton and smoke.

Her body is bruised violet,
violated. Corpse-cold?

All taxis taken, of course.
A hawker passes, passes.

No phone, no money,
I shout nothing back

at the sky, across
the endless sun-dressed steppe.

No echo.

*

No blood, no note. Patrick calling and calling:
not in the immaculate tub,

not in bed in a mood—all 95 pounds of her
hanging among their winter coats.

Her stomach's still warm.
I could hardly hear

my brother three states away,
trying to pry open a mouth.

When the ambulance took her,
no one wanted to sit or stay

standing. And the next day the morgue,
reading the report.

Thank god for my aunt who believes in heaven,
toasts to those we know there.

That tight-lipped Thanksgiving even my mom got tipsy:
the lilies were too close to the feast.

*

Three turkeys to eat and the wild ones
out there in the snow, how they carry on

when the smallest wanders off.

*

What I write down
I'll remember. What will happen
is happening already.
Can one worry a fear away?
The worst occurred
by surprise. A person beyond
ruined by a single morning:
over, erased, ashes
in the blue urn on the mantle
transferred to a Ziploc
inside a suitcase
carried across continents.
Nothing like a ruin tourists visit:
floor joist, plumbing part,
a pistol cemented
into the foundation.
Here nothing's left but the smell of her.
In the vacuum bag and drains
strands of her hair.

*

The opposite of displacement:
feeling too tied to that house,
and this one an ocean away.

The more pressing need is
to find the place I belonged—
or thought I belonged—changed:

different birds organizing the morning,
no full-length mirror in the foyer.
I worry more about not escaping

than shape or architecture,
whatever succulent can survive
the summer in the window box.

*

Before my friend moves closer in
slightly farther away from me, the distance

between bereaved and not, alive
and gone—I don't say I don't care

to the limitless questions circling your split life
or how overburdened to the point of slouching

you must have been, as I am in Safeway,
left on earth.

*

Patrick takes his last trip to Ulaanbaatar
to share the ashes with your sisters

who are no longer part of our family
—dead to us, to put it bluntly,

as you become harder to love,

a fact I fight against
like the slow erosion of our

yard, at first imperceptible;
even the bamboo, flattened

then up again the next day

greener, can't prevent
the memory of you

from loosening its grip.

*

My closet's a walk-in. I stand here
considering how you did it—

the mind divorced from the body entirely—
under my moth-eaten Mongolian dress,

a curvier version of the one we burned you in.
More sexy, you said, when we watched your sister

stitch the front slit closed for the Nadaam races.
When the near winner (only eight years old)

fell from his horse and they swept up his body—
Luck, you said, meaning fate in your awful English.

Or did you mean luck?
For a second I catch a shimmer of you

where the light switch should be,
your voice like moth wings beating down the door,

on edge, always on the edge of answering.

On Happiness

Before I was born, my father went away
& forgot me. When I was old enough

my mother let me fold clothes:
sock puppets over my hands

talking to me, objects I could scold.
No, no, no. I was terrified

by the afternoons but knew
not to wake her or shut the window

to the garden. Words only I heard
in the gluey dollhouse,

down the hallway like a sea
I learned about in school,

Baltic, Bering, Dead—windless
as the trees against the bluest sky

a sky could manage. In the picture
I looked happy, squatting on the grass,

my bony knees in my arms.

Twachtman's Springtime

Seen through the wavy glass
even the farmhouse disappears.

A black birch in the distance
smeared across the pond,

which I might call swollen,
depending on how long it had stormed,

how nauseating the lilacs just after.
It's either dusk or very early morning:

ground and sky bleed into each other.
The painting's more interested in weather

than love or justice, the fog being the only
alive thing.

Blossom Road

I don't know why I pulled over, idling, right before Christmas,
    two months of snow and salt
plowed onto the shoulder, each squat rambler aglow, a life-size
    baby Jesus reborn in the DiPasquale's front yard,
why everything looked different, the way the woods you got lost
    in as a kid seem small and disappointing when you return to
    them older,
because I hadn't been out of there that long, less than a year,
    and as far as I could tell in the December blur,
beyond the slight expansion of the motherhouse infirmary,
    where the sick nuns, most of them retired teachers,
convalesced or passed, where I'd volunteered during study hall
    changing bedpans and pouring Hawaiian Punch into paper
    cups,
they hadn't renovated the spired building I'd entered day after
    day, my plaid jumper becoming more ironic with each curve.
How selfish it is after you leave a place to doubt that it could
    function without you.
That it all goes on was enough to make me crack, facing the
    grotto
I'd stood around with my class, a hundred of us, in Easter
    white in another season,
singing as the May queen and her court offered flowers to the
    stone Virgin or just pretending to sing.

IV.

Summer in Kittery

For pity, for the passerby who might point, I'm wafting around in a nightgown.

When did winter become rain in sheets, August, the lilies unwither themselves?

How they open to overwhelm the others that give in, tired of night, of lasting.

The ocean dulled, gull-less, nobody's passed, not a single dinghy—I look through it for too long

for the man who, come dawn, will set himself on fire by the shipyard.

A woman watching, I'll read in the paper later, will mistake the gasoline poured over his head for seawater.

What I can't see in this dark I know from memory: honey locust, stray, wait-a-bit

thorn, then Nate glowing from darts, a few drinks, the moon's residue on the shirt that looks like Easter.

I feel for the missing button halfway across a bridge dividing two states—no, bringing them together.

Dolor Notebook

1. THE SHAPE OF TANS TO COME

A pineapple isosceles and a little brittle umbrella.
Already you've had enough poolside

piña coladas for someone your size.
Boca Chica—the only hotel with a vacancy

when you pulled in at some crepuscular hour.
Little Mouth. Your own feels big—

warm with rum—though you've kept quiet.
A lot has changed since '68,

the brink of Acapulco's decline—
your impression of it lifted from the old *Life*

you found at a flea market: two leggy starlets
in asymmetrical black, their blond hair bobbed,

their bellies bare. That was before we understood
the danger of ultraviolet rays,

before we developed ways to keep
the almost (should-be) dead alive.

2. FINALE OF SEEM

Most likely you were beside yourself in the "Healing Garden,"
hidden among plastic bamboo, when his vitals started failing—

the light was brilliant, holy. Despite the signs forbidding it
you lit your last Camel only to watch it burn clear to the filter.

The cardiac residents said he would go quickly,
without pain, once they upped the morphine,

but when his death finally made it to the clipboard,
he'd been dying—raging against it—for days.

In the last hour, you'd whispered something
hopeful into his ear. At the top of his lungs (filled with fluid)

he'd yelled—impossibly—back, "Don't you think I know that?"

3. PIMLICO

You try to block it out with small distractions:
at a horse track, sitting cross-legged in the grass

while Roger Daltrey gyrates, you're too aware
of your age to do more than chug a skunked beer.

For the first time in a long time
that ache just under your ribs

hasn't come from sex, the vulnerable
position of the sun, the cumulus rush.

A stranger takes a picture of your breasts—
you glimpse them in his viewfinder seconds later:

voyeur to your own body. No, you aren't angry
or ashamed, you feel no need to punch his face.

Yes, if he'd like, he could post it on the Net.

4. UNSET SUNSET

Waking fully clothed to the lamp on, the bulb hot,
you can't remember drifting off, but as you busied yourself

moving stacks of books to a more manageable corner,
you returned to that not-yet night near Barnegat,

just a bathroom break on the coastal route to New York,
the sun like a fruit bruised above the ocean.

Nate bought Cheetos; you made another expected metaphor
out of it, the dissolution both messy and intricate, fast

and slow. Then more talk about endings, about memory's
inaccuracy, how, looking back, that specific shade of sky

would seem less real, less rare. Under your breath,
barely audible against the surf, you got everything wrong.

Lovebird

Caged a few stops away, convinced
that the image she bangs her wings

against each morning is something
other, better, than her own:

her long-gone mate Pete! Every day
the same, mouthing millet.

You envy her bird mirror,
her bird heart. You want to touch

the cheek of a complete stranger
across the aisle, but when the bus halts,

it's your own wet face you hold.
According to the sky—a cloudless

blue piercing—everything's dandy.
You step onto the street haunted

as usual by its name, Gallows,
walk the half-mile to the hospital

humming a song that won't help
the man on the third floor dissolve

into his cot or the woman losing him,
swabbing his nose, the nose you have,

with oil. And when you ask how he's doing—
"The same. I'm dead or I'm dying."

Widow

Out of stray toothpicks and paper chewed off jars,
even mice build nests, make themselves

small enough to fit through cracks.
To envy the things she'd invested in killing!

When she found one in rigor mortis,
it took the steel spatula to free him from the floor

and stuck with her the whole walk to wherever she never
noticed the meteor shower.

Fallow, she heard in her head. *Quick!*
Before you turn fallow.

That day she had to lie down laughter left.
Without it, she felt estranged. (Bored sick.)

In the alleyway, late spring, two, maybe three
feral cats wait for scraps,

the only flowers still alive she's dreamed:
how somebody's mother stood on the porch at dawn

fumbling with the hose.
If she could afford it, she'd find a condo

overlooking the park, more resilient to rain:
bricks tuck-pointed, tin roof. No more morning chores.

Lately she's as forgettable
as her box elder, deemed by the city a weed

rotting from the inside. Or wanting—
unable to open the mail—to be hermetic.

Too much asphalt. Fault. Her husband's heart faltered.
And when his face lost color, they covered it with a pall.

Mouths moved to greet her saying dumb comforting things
as though underwater or she was—

wondering out loud in the flooded crawl space
about "ultimate disposal," the mousy grief

counselor's words. Not hers.

On Gardening and Geeshie Wiley

Gardening's not my thing
but I've memorized
the list of prohibited invasives
in line for my dump permit
ready to purge, let go of what's
accumulating in the corners.
Maybe I'll downsize, relocate
to a houseboat moored
in the Piscataqua. To stand
right there in the middle
of the river and see my face
from the other side
in both places at once or nowhere—
like the blues singer bellowing
through my headphones
about motherlessness
or my own mother
insisting no, I don't know
a loss that looming,
that primal, as the snow
blanketed our car
and I hoped the woods
abutting her childhood home
would fill up with it, swallow us,
the woods she hid inside,
hand-pulling tree-of-heaven
from the stone wall
before the plant could seed,
then digging up the terrible roots.

Not Going to Nova Scotia

Instead I'll stay put on this peninsula
against a backdrop of yacht rock

and boxed wine while you, love,
want only to be stranded

on some northern cove without amenities
or prior knowledge of the tides, even more alive

in chaos. When will we build
the widow's walk you call a crow's nest—

what's the difference?—the lookout
from which I'll wait like Pound's

river-merchant's wife, writing
her dead letters, my small hand

a visor barely weakening the sun
when you return unhurt in August.

Epithalamion For Nate

What is space?
I asked you once. Silence.

We are an argument—years—
beyond le béguin, our fiery beginning.

I mean I need you here and away.
At Seapoint days ago

the sky was just sun
so I dove into the waves.

When the ache in my legs left
I kicked farther out and watched you

doze or maybe you were reading
on the shore. Your back to me

I knew where your gaze was going:
a small gull tottering

one-legged in the reeds.
How long can we grieve?

It's not that we get better
—we are able to stand more.

For Bourgeois, the most important part
was always the spine,

what it can bear over a lifetime.

Sunset Redux

Darkness doesn't descend suddenly at all.
Even the most severe shifts of cloud

and color are hard to track, we don't notice
a huge change happening till it's over.

When exactly did the honey-colored band burst,
the pink mouth melt to nothing?

When you put your hand over his,
over the bright red light of his fingertip (pulse ox)

he asked, *Am I dead? Am I dead?* Maybe more than twice
when you caught yourself laughing, let his hand go.

Postcard from Mazunte

Somehow Peter, Paul & Mary are still singing.
Hundreds of miles by car, not rail,
with a brand new timing belt, a tent, luck—
though we found worms in the orange juice
and for eight days straight
we've been unable to eat.
This is not a landscape I know:
loud, unidentifiable birds, the coast
yielding to mountains, mangroves, our palapa
peppered with hyacinth. Here, when he touches me
I feel the Pacific swell, everything swirling inside.
There's no disembodiment: I am my hips
moving above him, my chest caving in;
that strange sound I make is mine.
At Zipolite, we swim naked, unafraid of drowning
as far as the current will pull us.
This *a-way*. This *a-way*. This far away from grief.

ACKNOWLEDGMENTS

My sincerest thanks to the editors of the following journals in which poems from this collection first appeared, often in altered versions: *Blackbird; Conjunctions Online; Forklift, Ohio; Gulf Coast; H_NGM_N; Oversound;* and *Tikkun.*

To the faculty and students in the English Department at the University of Maryland for nurturing my creative spirit.

To Jennifer Chang, my first creative writing teacher, for seeing my false Polaris, and to my tireless teachers after, all of whom have marked this book: Michael Collier, Rita Dove, Brigit Pegeen Kelly, Stanley Plumly, Jean Valentine, Joshua Weiner, and Rachel Wetzsteon.

To Elizabeth Arnold and Lisa McCullough, my closest readers, for the inspiration of their work and the deadlines.

To Danielle Cadena Deulen for believing wholeheartedly in this collection and for her supreme editorial vision.

To Samuel Amadon, Maud Casey, Liz Countryman, Christina Duhig, Kelly Forsythe, Sofi Hall, Laura Leichum, Gerald Maa, L. S. McKee, Katherine DeBlassie Page, and Hannah Baker Saltmarsh for their friendship, encouragement, and guidance through this book's long birth.

To Paul Guest, Beth Dial, the National Poetry Series, and everyone at the University of Georgia Press, especially Jon Davies and Beth Snead, for giving *What It Doesn't Have to Do With* such a lovely home.

To April Gornik for *Virga*.

To my parents; my brothers, Patrick and Mark; and my grandmother Judy Sullivan Bernal for putting up with me the longest.

Above all, thank you, Nate: you helped the most.

NOTES

"Heartbroken in Your Memoir" is for Danielle Cadena Deulen.

"Postcard from Long Island City" is for Theresa McCaul.

"Interrogation after The Cremaster Cycle" refers to the five films and the site-specific installation by Matthew Barney at the Guggenheim in 2003.

"Postcard from the Villa Catullo" reimagines—and lifts phrases from—Ezra Pound's "Blandula, Tenulla, Vagula." The italicized question (*What do I love and where are you?*) is from Pound's "Notes for Canto CXVII et seq."

A Lume Spento, mentioned in a later section of "Venice Is Sinking," is the title of Pound's first collection of poems. "Venice Is Sinking" also draws from *The Pisan Cantos*.

"What It Doesn't Have to Do With" references Modest Mouse's album *Building Nothing Out of Something*, released in 2000.

"The Story of Our Estrangement" and "No Echo" are for Patrick T. Bernal. The italicized line in "The Story of Our Estrangement" (*Today's Tom Sawyer he gets high on you*) is from the song "Tom Sawyer" by Rush, released in 1981 on the album *Moving Pictures*.

"On Happiness" is for Teresa Matula Bobrow and began as an erasure of two pages from Jenny Offill's novel *Last Things* (New York: Vintage Contemporaries, 1999).

"Dolor Notebook," "Lovebird," and "Sunset Redux" are in memory of William P. Bernal Sr. (1920–2006). The title of the second section of "Dolor Notebook" ("Finale of Seem") is from "The Emperor of Ice-Cream" by Wallace Stevens.

"On Gardening and Geeshie Wiley" is in memory of Mildred Matula Allyn (1924–2010).

The italicized sentence in "Epithalamion for Nate" (*It's not that we get better / —we are able to stand more.*) is from Donald Kuspit's interview with Louise Bourgeois in *Bourgeois*, Elizabeth Avedon Editions (New York: Vintage Books, 1988).

The italicized words in "Postcard from Mazunte" (*This a-way. This a-way*) are from Peter, Paul & Mary's version of the folk song "500 Miles."

www.ingramcontent.com/pod-product-compliance
Lightning Source LLC
Chambersburg PA
CBHW010927180426
43192CB00043B/2788